CRUSH YOUR COMPETITION MARKETING STRATEGIES FOR CONTRACTORS

OUT OF THE BOX MARKETING TACTICS FOR SMALL SERVICE BUSINESSES

By Barry Maddox Jr.

Disclaimer

The information provided in this book is meant
to provide helpful information on the subjects
discussed. The publisher and author are not
responsible for any financial needs that may
require professional services and are not liable
for any damages or negative consequences
from any strategy, action, application or
preparation to any person reading or following
the information provided in this book.
References are provided for informational
purposes only and do not constitute
endorsement of any websites or other sources.

TABLE OF CONTENTS

PREFACE

This book is full of Crush Your Competition non-traditional marketing tips that will help you generate more profits. It's based on marketing strategies that I have used in my own exterior cleaning business that I started over a decade ago. These tactics will work for many different types of small businesses. Businesses such as painting, lawn care, landscaping, carpet cleaning, pressure washing, window cleaning, maid services, remodeling, roofing, gutter cleaning, tree trimming, snow plowing, dirt work, concrete work, duct cleaning, insulation, chimney sweeping, plumbing, siding, installations, dry walling, contracting, HVAC, irrigation, deck building, handyman, babysitting, pet sitting or walking, and many other services. Any business that provides homeowner type services will benefit greatly from these surefire marketing methods that will crush your competition. You can begin to implement these strategies instantly to start generating more profit from your existing or new start up service business. These effective strategies can be used to add many new customers and to build a solid customer base. This book reveals secrets that you don't want your competitors knowing.

CHAPTER 1. WHY TRADITIONAL MARKETING EATS PROFITS

What is Marketing? Look up the definition of marketing if you want but in simple terms, marketing is anything you do that promotes, advertises, communicates, represents, targets or highlights your company. Marketing is different from advertising, which is a specific form of marketing. Advertising can be print ads like postcards, newspaper or magazine ads, or a phone book listing. Advertising can also be broadcasted through radio or TV ads. Pay per click ads are another form of advertising. Marketing however is *anything* that portrays your company. Marketing is all the forms of advertising mentioned above plus your company's website, vehicle lettering, apparel, social media, letterheads, logo, yard signs and even your voicemail message. Marketing is everything you do that promotes your company in any way, shape, or form. It is the channel of anything and everything you use to tell the world about your company.

Traditional Marketing. Most of us are familiar with traditional marketing strategies. Perhaps you've tried a few of them or currently still are. I am in no way dismissing any of the following types of marketing or saying they can't work. Phone books, direct mailing, radio, and TV ads can work without a doubt, but they're expensive. The more effective and less expensive tactics revealed in this book can be used to increase profits compared to non-traditional more expensive methods if you put in a little work. Traditional ways of marketing drive up your customer acquisition costs (CAC). That is the cost it takes to acquire a new customer. The problem is that most small businesses don't track this number. All they care about is that the phone rings and they keep the schedule full. But then at the end of the year they wonder where all the money went.

CAC is calculated by adding up all the costs spent to acquire a new customer divided by the number of customers acquired during that period. For example, if a company spends $1000 on marketing a month and acquires 10 customers that month directly from that marketing, their CAC is $100. It costs them $100 to gain one customer. This cost is then figured in with all other expenses like fuel, employees, insurance, and materials associated with a job. For example, if a painter acquires a new customer and lands a job to paint two bedrooms for $500, that $100 CAC means his profit from that job is already down to $400. Bid ($500) – ($100) CAC = ($400) profit. Then all the other expenses are factored in as well. You can begin to see what looked like a $500 job may actually only net a couple hundred bucks. That's why it is so important to keep your CAC down by using outside the box, less expensive, but very effective marketing tactics.

The yellow pages are a great example of "traditional marketing." Prior to the Internet, the yellow pages were one of the few places potential customers could find services. Yet even today yellow page representatives make ridiculous claims and promises. They tell you the bigger your ad, the more your phone will ring. Some business owners actually name their company so it's the first listing people see on the page like AAA Automotive for example. Yellow page ads are an expensive form of advertising and therefore drive up CAC and drive profits down. What I've found is that having an honorable mention in the phone book, (which is normally free by the way) is more than enough for the few amount of customers it might bring me. The Internet has pretty much made phone books and yellow pages worthless in my opinion. After all, when was the last time you looked for a service in the yellow page book?

Traditional direct mailing methods can be just as ineffective. I know a handyman who used to send out around 20,000 postcards every spring to his surrounding service area. The cost for having these postcards designed, printed, and mailed was approximately $10,000 or .50 cents per postcard. He used the jumbo-sized cards because they stood out more than the smaller standard size. At an average of 1% call back rate, he would land around half of those jobs. So he basically gained 100 new customers, give or take, from his postcard campaign. Not factoring in any other expenses like gas for doing the estimates or daily operating costs, he was looking at an initial CAC of $100 per customer. If the job was large enough, say a couple thousand dollars, then it was feasible. But his average job was $300-$400. That means on a $300 job he still had the $100 CAC cutting into his profits. After paying for fuel, insurance, and employee wages, he was actually losing money on some jobs.

High advertising costs aren't sustainable and can be a recipe for disaster. It's true he could have looked for ways to cut expenses. He could have found cheaper postcard services or raised his prices, but the point I'm trying to make is that starting out with a high CAC puts you at a disadvantage right out of the gate. I remember talking to him midway through the season as he was bragging about how busy he was and how many jobs he had booked. But when the dust settled at the end of the year, the profits weren't there and he eventually had to downsize and rethink his marketing strategies. Now, using some of the Crush Your Competition Marketing Strategies in this book he has made a nice comeback.

CHAPTER 2. RADIUS BLAST MARKETING

What I call radius blast marketing (RBM) is a simple, low cost marketing strategy that I use on a regular basis. Its effectiveness and return on investment (ROI) is unmatched compared to most traditional methods. I don't claim to have invented this marketing technique but I have tweaked it over the years and made it my own. This marketing tactic basically targets neighbors of customers.

How it works. Whenever I land a job I will observe the neighborhood. Most of my exterior cleaning jobs are in nice subdivisions or small neighborhoods. If I'm there servicing one homeowner there is a good chance others in the neighborhood would hire me as well. If the neighborhood looks like it has potential, I will mark on that particular job sheet to implement radius blast marketing. I will simply write RBM at the top of the job sheet. Once the job is complete I wait for the customer's approval and payment. Once all is good, and we've created another happy customer, I pull the trigger. I, or more often now my secretary, will pull that job sheet out of the accounts receivable file and see the RBM note at the top.

We get the addresses of neighbors around that job. We basically draw a radius around that address, hence "radius blast marketing." We most commonly use whitepages.com. Enter that homeowner's address then scroll to the bottom and click *"see more neighbors in this area."* This will bring up a map of more addresses in the radius of the job you did. Copy and paste or manually type these addresses into a mailing label document. We just address it to "Resident" and enter the street, city, and zip below that. The mailing labels I use are 1" x 2 5/8" and there are 30 labels per sheet. To fill up the entire sheet we will find and enter at least 30 addresses or even 60 or 90 if it's a big neighborhood. This way we don't waste any labels. Stick the labels on an equal amount of envelopes. The next step is to write a letter in a word document to mail to each address. You'll only have to write the letter once then save it to reuse each time. An example of my letter is as follows:

Dear Valued Homeowner,

My name is (full name), owner of (company name). I realize your time is valuable so I will keep this short. We have recently been working in your neighborhood and I wanted to introduce my company and myself. Your neighbors, the Harrison's at 5555 Tulip Court, recently hired us to wash their house and driveway. Because you are a nearby neighbor, we wanted to extend this service to you, as well as our other services. We know that it can be difficult to find a contractor that you can trust, but being able to ask your neighbors about the service they received can help put your mind at ease. We offer free estimates and would love the opportunity to meet you and discuss your exterior cleaning needs. As you probably know, mold and mildew can cause serious health problems. These contaminants are present on most houses in your neighborhood and can get into the home through open windows, vented soffits, and attic vents. We can kill and remove these harmful pollutants to make your home safe, restore its appearance, and help boost curb appeal and value. Our work is backed by our exclusive guarantee, "The Most Detailed Exterior Cleaning Ever Or It's FREE." For more information, customer testimonials, pictures of our work, or to request an estimate online, please visit (website). Thank you so much for your time; we look forward to hearing from you.

I then finalize it by putting "Sincerely," my name, company name, and phone number. I also add my company logo to the signature and the day's date. Use a formal letter format on Word and make it look professional. Break it up into paragraphs and tweak it to fit your business. Once you save it then all you have to do is change the customer name, address, services performed and date for each new campaign. From there we tri fold the letters and stuff them into each envelope along with a business card. Then simply stamp and mail them. You can put return labels on them as well but it isn't necessary. You will get a few returned to you once in a while but that doesn't matter. Normally the reason is a vacant home. When we get returns we'll open them up and save the business card.

Now what's so great about sending out 30 letters you say? Well here is my philosophy as to why it works so well. Even with only 30 letters I will usually get 1-3 calls. That's more than a 3% rate of return (ROR) on the low end. Considering the average direct mail campaign is a ½ to 2 percent ROR, that's pretty good. Being conservative let's say I only got one call from say 60 letters, that's still a high average. Even better news is that I can usually close 80-90 percent of those new calls. Again, that is a very high percentage. Here is where the sales letter works its magic. People may not know my company or me, but they trust their neighbors. Let me say that again. People trust their neighbors! In a tight knit community like a subdivision, people will use the same contractors that their neighbors are using. Perhaps they know the Harrison's we worked for, or at least know of them. Maybe they know that side street is right over there in their neighborhood and that makes them feel safe in hiring us. It makes us credible so to speak. It gives us merit. They can even go talk to the Harrison's if they know them, and that's only a plus because remember, the Harrison's were happy with our services. Just be sure to keep your prices consistent in case neighbors do talk.

So they call, I give them a fair price and close them 80-90 percent of the time. In addition, I find that once I land a job from a letter, I can repeat my radius blast to target different neighbors and add the name of two customers to the letter. For example, *"we recently did work for both the Harrison's and the Peterson's."* Mentioning two different homeowners adds even more credibility. To figure my costs on the letters I add in everything including the cost of the envelopes, paper, ink, labels, business cards, stamps, and the hourly rate for my secretary doing all the work. On average, each letter costs me around one dollar. To send out 30 letters at $1 apiece I'm spending $30. Again being conservative, if I acquire only one customer from a 30-letter campaign, I have a CAC of $30. Now a $300-$400 job results a lot more profit. I'm adding $70 in pure profit over the previously mentioned $100 CAC example. Say I land 50 jobs over the entire year from the sales letter, that extra $70 adds a whopping $3500 to my bottom line. At 100 jobs, it adds $7,000. It's easy to see how this one marketing campaign can be way more profitable over an expensive yellow page ad or a traditional direct mailing campaign. The numbers may not be exact for every company but you get the point. It's more profitable and gets a better ROI than most traditional marketing tactics if you actually pay attention to the numbers. Plus, it's super easy to do and it's something you can start implementing right now.

CHAPTER 3. CREATE A BLOG

The Internet is responsible for the most drastic change in marketing in history. Traditional marketing tactics are outdated and expensive. If you still use them they should at least be supplemented with a strong Internet presence.

Have a Website. I'm going to assume your company has a website. If not, you're missing out. The Internet is a wonderful source of customer leads, which equals profits. For under $10 you can buy a domain name. When I first started my company in 2005 I made sure the company name I chose was available as a dot COM web domain. I'm not going to spend a bunch of time on the specifics of a website other than if you don't have one, get one! Also go for a dot COM address if available and if not, use a dot NET. For a few hundred dollars you can have a website designed. Be sure it looks professional, is informative, and is optimized with keywords. It should have as much content on it as possible without sounding like spam or looking too cluttered. Also be sure it has a "request an estimate" form. Customers like the convenience of requesting an estimate online, plus it frees up your phone lines. On average, I receive half of my leads via the phone and half through my online estimate form.

Unfortunately, I know so many small companies that still don't have a website. I can tell you if you don't think you need one, you're wrong, if you want to gain more leads that is. It isn't hard to get your website ranking locally for keywords related to your industry. My company is based in a small town of about 12,000 people. There are some more populated areas within an hour's drive that I serve but no large major cities. I still get a lot of traffic to my site and requests for estimates. My industry is pressure washing, yes, pressure washing, and I still get a ton of leads and make thousands of dollars in profit every year through my website. So if you provide any type of homeowner targeted service (or commercial work for that matter), in any part of the country, you need to have a website. Hopefully if you're reading this you've got the website thing covered or will have very soon.

Have a Blog. The Crush Your Competition Marketing Strategy here is to become a blogger. A blogger? Yes, a blogger but don't run off just yet, here me out. A blog by definition is a regularly updated website or web page that is written in an informal or conversational style. Why do I need a blog you're asking? A blog will help your website rank better, meaning it will show up in the search engines better. A blog is a powerful tool that most small businesses don't utilize. This is where you are going to gain the edge over your competition. I highly recommend having the blog integrated into your website. Don't make it a separate web address. Have a web design company add it right into your site. I also highly recommend using the WordPress format. It's the most popular and by far the easiest one to customize. Have the blog customized to look like the rest of your website. When people click on the *"blog"* or *"articles"* tab, depending on what you call it, the page should look like the rest of your site. The side menus should look the same, the header banner up top the same, colors, font type and size, etc. This way it blends right in with your site.

The advantage of having a blog is to add fresh content to your website on a consistent basis. Search engines love fresh and frequent content. To help you understand this concept more clearly, let's look at how search engines work. I'll keep this simple and won't get into a bunch of confusing algorithms. When a potential customer goes to Google or any search engine where they type in what they're looking for, the search results show pages that are most relevant to their search. The more relevant the page the higher it will rank. By relevance I mean the keywords used in the search match keywords on that particular page. That's why I suggested having as much content on your website as possible, and be sure it's optimized with your industries keywords.

Other elements like a webpage's ranking, domain age, locality, and competitiveness of the search term are also factored in but for the most part it's relevant keywords that hold the most power. I can tell you people type in some strange searches and you'll never be able to cover them all with a static website. In addition, not everyone will type in the same search. I studied keyword searches and search engine optimization for several years to get my website to rank well. At first my website did not have a blog, but it was about 15 pages long and was very informative. This not only helped to educate potential customers but it also gave me some space to stuff in a ton of keywords. Even with all that, there were still search results I wasn't showing up for but some of my competition was. This pissed me off to say the least after all the time and money I had spent building my website. But I learned it's nearly impossible to stuff all your industry's long tailed keywords into 15 pages or less without it being cluttered or spammy. Furthermore, most small business websites are only 8 pages or less, giving them less space. This is where a blog will put your company on another level.

How it works. With a blog you can create short articles to purposely target keyword searches. For example, let's say I'm a painter in Springfield and my website wasn't ranking well for a particular keyword term like *"painting contractors in Springfield",* I could write an article literally titled Painting Contractors in Springfield. The main body of the article would talk about; you guessed it, painting contractors in Springfield. It should make sense and be informative but you don't have to get all technical or over anal about it. Just write a nice article in a conversational format that's informative and use those keywords in that order at least 3 or 4 times, as well as in different variations. Don't over stuff keywords or it will sound like spam. On average, the articles should be around 300-400 words long.

After writing the article and proofreading, I click publish and presto, I have essentially created a new page on my website that will rank for its relevant keywords. Now when someone local types the search *"painting contractors in Springfield",* that new page is likely to show up once Google indexes it. It will get indexed the next time Google pings your website. "Ping" means they stop by to see how things are going and to see if there is anything new. If so, the fresh content gets indexed and will now start showing in search results. How often your site gets pinged depends on how often there is updated content. If you have a small static website that just sits there, they may only ping it every few weeks or so, but once you start adding fresh content regularly, they'll ping it more often. At one time I was adding new content so often that whenever I posted a new blog article it would start showing up in the search results within minutes. It was like Google was just sitting there at my doorstep waiting for me to throw out some fresh content. But regardless, eventually your new article will get indexed and start ranking.

Each time you write an article, you create a new webpage on your site that will show up for relevant search terms. What this means is you can purposely target specific keywords for services you provide, specific cities you serve, and many different combinations of each. Now if someone searches *painting contractors, painting companies, painting services, or painting business* combined with a particular city, you've got it covered in all the articles you've written. You should add city names you serve in the title and article body. I've also learned to put zip codes of areas I serve in articles because people search that way as well. You can see how you could easily create an endless amount of articles targeting keyword search terms in variations of all the services you provide with city names, without cites names, with zip codes, etc. You could never target all of them with an 8-15 page static website. Now you have potential customers landing on your website that wouldn't have found you before. It doesn't matter how they get there, whether it's an article you wrote, or they found your homepage, what matters is that they found you. They may or may not read the article, but now they are free to browse your site and hopefully initiate contact. In addition, the articles make your company seem like an authority and that you know what you're talking about.

As mentioned, search engines love fresh content. So if you're writing articles on a regular basis, the search engines pick up on that. The extra benefit is it helps your whole website to rank better because they know the content is fresh and updated. That's why you may have noticed that you used to rank well for a search term but don't anymore. That's because the article is out dated and other competing webpages have since showed up and now they are over ranking you. Like previously mentioned, when you write an article on your blog, it creates a completely new page on your site. So this essentially increases the size of your website. Search engines see bigger websites as authorities and may rank their pages above a smaller websites page even if it's just as relevant. My website started out at 15 pages when it first went live, now, with all the articles I've written, it's a 2,400 page website!

A blog is the way to go if you want to show up in the search results for your industry's keywords. This marketing tactic has easily made me thousands of dollars and has helped me build a huge customer base, which leads to lots of repeat and referral work. Best of all, once you put in the work, your customer acquisition costs (CAC) are fairly low. After the initial cost of adding a blog to your site, writing articles yourself is FREE. You'll rank well locally, customers will find you, and you'll increase your profits. It's really that simple and effective! I know some of you reading this will be intimidated by the thought of writing articles. But I'm telling you it isn't difficult. WordPress is very easy to use, that's why it's so popular. You can even outsource the article writing if you want to.

Be Warned. DO NOT copy any content off the Internet and use it for your own articles. Search engines will detect the duplicate content and will red flag your website, possibly removing it from the search results completely. Make sure the content you use is unique.

CHAPTER 4. OFFER A GUARANTEE

In this final section I'm going to reveal several more marketing strategies. These aren't easily measurable in terms of an exact return on your investment like the radius blast marketing but in my opinion they're priceless.

Create a Guarantee. One of the best things I did for my company was to implement a guarantee. If one of your customers asked you if you have a guarantee on your work, what would you say? Think about it and try to answer honestly. If you don't have an immediate solid answer then it's fair to say you don't have a guarantee. You need to be creative here and come up with one that fits your company. I'm not talking the traditional *"100% satisfaction guarantee"* either. Everyone has that and in my opinion, customers look right past it, meaning it has no value. I created one that says, *"The Most Detailed Exterior Cleaning Ever Or It's FREE."* I borrowed the idea from a marketing book I read and tweaked it for exterior cleaning. I then made up a separate logo that had that saying on it and now it's on my business cards, website, and even my company vehicles.

I know what you're thinking. You don't want to be doing a bunch of jobs for free because you didn't live up to the promise, right? Wrong! I was worried at first too but I've never had a single customer ask for their money back or for a freebie because it wasn't the most detailed. I'm sure somewhere out there, there is that one customer that's just looking to take advantage but it's rare and they'll find a way to take advantage of you anyway if that's the type of person they are. The amount of profit generated just from having that guarantee and marketing it like I do is priceless. People like the boldness of it. It portrays my company's confidence and ability to do quality work. It gets them believing, even before we do any work at all, that we're going to do a great job. It works wonders and is something you should implement immediately. Use a similar version or make up your own. Just be creative and think out of the box.

Create a Warranty. This is different than a guarantee and can be used in addition to a guarantee. A few years back I got together with a couple of friends who were also successful exterior cleaning company owners. We got together just to brainstorm ideas over a long weekend. Some very profitable ideas emerged. I talked about how my guarantee had done so well and from that we created a warranty that fit our businesses. It's a *"2 Year No Mold Warranty,"* that basically guarantees no mold will return on the house siding or roof for 2 years after we clean it or we'll come back and clean it for free. Again, I created a logo and put it on all of my marketing. The best return was printing the logo on my estimate sheets right there with the price of the services. This helps sell value and allows me to charge more.

People love guarantees and warranties. They take comfort in knowing they are protected. I can't tell you how many times a customer called to accept an estimate and said, *"You weren't the cheapest but the others didn't offer any type of guarantee or warranty."* After we complete a warrantied job my secretary sends them a warranty certificate in the mail that they have to sign and send back within 30 days. We then file it until the 2 years is up. Similar to the guarantee I offer, I have never had a warranty claim. Most people just give us a call after 2-3 years to have us clean again and get covered under a new warranty. Come up with some type of warranty you can implement and market the heck out of it. Just be sure it fits into your parameters and that it's feasible. Don't warranty something that is impossible to keep your promise on.

Payment Convenience. You have to make it easy for your customers to do business with you. These days there are multiple ways for people to pay for services, yet I still see small service businesses that don't accept various ways of payment. I started accepting credit cards several years ago and it's been great. At first I cringed at the small percentage that the credit card merchant scrapes off the top but then I realized if someone couldn't pay for our services without putting it on a credit card, they probably wouldn't hire us anyway. This realization made it worth implementing and it's worked out well. With smart phones and tablets, there really isn't a reason you can't accept credit cards. I use Register, previously known as Square. The account was super easy to set up and the reader was free. It plugs right into my phone and is easy to use. Within a day or two the money is transferred to my business account. I just recently got the contactless and chip reader because that is quickly become the more secure and preferred method of payment over the traditional magnetic stripe cards.

Answering the Phone. Last but certainly not least, is the way you answer your phone and voicemail message when you can't pick up. If you think about it, this is the first contact a potential customer has with you or a representative of your company. Why wouldn't you want to take advantage of that? There is only so much you can say when you do answer the phone, but saying your company name and then waiting for them to reply is mediocre at best. I answer something like this, *"Hello, thank you for calling (company name), this is Barry, how can I help?"* I say it with a smile on my face. I know that sounds odd because they can't actually see me but when you smile while you speak, it comes off more enthusiastic. I normally get a reply like, *"well hello Barry, yes I was wondering if I could get an estimate on…"* Now they feel special. They feel like I actually care (which I do) and that first impression is huge! Another tip I use is to write their name down immediately after they say it so I don't forget it. Then at the very end of the conversation I'll be sure to call them by name and thank them. Again, I'm making them feel important because in fact they are.

My voicemail is quite a bit different. Obviously I have a little more time to speak before they hear the tone indicating it's time for them to speak. I take full advantage of this opportunity and build credibility. My voicemail to date goes like this with a smile, *"Thank you for calling (company name), the exterior cleaning professionals serving northern Indiana for over a decade. Our normal business hours are M-F 8-4; if we've missed your call during these hours we're most likely helping another customer. Please leave your name, number and a brief message and we will call you back with our quick callback guarantee. In the meantime, you can visit us at (website) for more information or to request an estimate. Thank you and we look forward to talking with you shortly."* I can't tell you how many times I've listened to a customer's voicemail that starts out by saying, *"man I really love your message."* Positive feedback like that is priceless and tells me I'm doing things right. Try implementing something like this into your phone message.

CONCLUSION

I hope you've enjoyed reading this book. I know you'll put some, if not all of these marketing strategies into action. If so, I guarantee you'll increase your profits. I think it will also help open your mind a little to other "out of the box" type marketing tactics. I truly find that it isn't that hard to stay a notch above your competition if you're creatively determined to succeed. I've found that just being honest and punctual with customers goes a long way in creating a successful business. Most of all, sell value, sell the end result, sell a solution to a problem and you'll go much further than someone selling on price or being deceptive. I'll also tell you that your business will continue to grow if you regularly question everything you do. In other words, look for a better, quicker, more efficient, and profitable way to do everything in your business. Question your own systems and ways of doing things. Don't get stuck in a rut and have that, *"oh we've always done it that way so that's just how we do it,"* attitude. Stay creative and find ways to be more efficient, because time is money. Upgrade your processes, polish your professionalism, take a step back and look at your company's image once in a while. See what your customers see from every aspect and then fix or hone whatever your weakest areas are. Do this and you'll beat the odds. You'll build a huge customer base and be able to rely on word of mouth, referral, and repeat work keeping your acquisition costs low and your profits high. Thanks again and until next time, keep your foot on the pedal.

www.ingramcontent.com/pod-product-compliance
Lightning Source LLC
Chambersburg PA
CBHW070424190526
45169CB00003B/1407